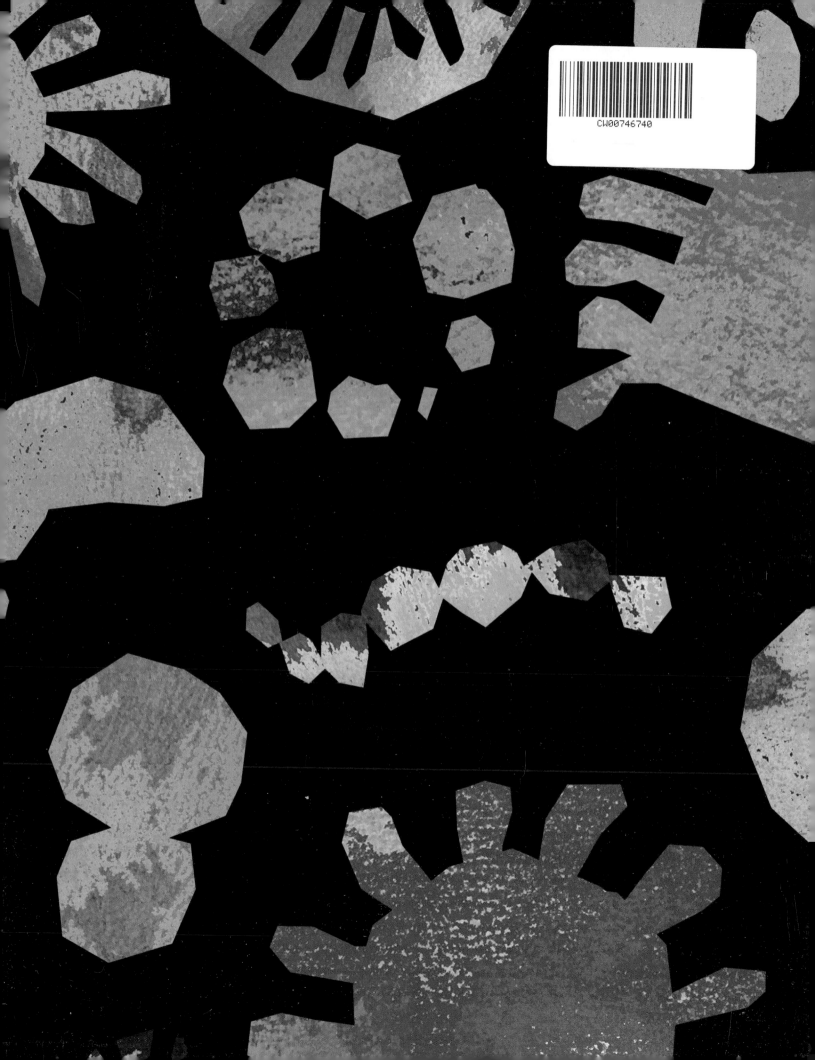

What others had to say about *Gran's Guide to Good Guts – My Friend Mikey*

"I love this book and I am excited as I know it will have a place in my teachings. Who better than a grandmother to help children learn how to feel better! Job well done!"

Virginia Harper, Digestive Healing for Life. USA.

"This will work well with families who are trying to make changes; it is an enjoyable book for schools to support learning about the digestive system."

Sandra Denton, Deputy Head Teacher, East Sussex.

"It's a lovely book and the information inside is medically accurate. I am happy to endorse it."

Dr Adrian Grigore, General Practitioner, East Sussex.

"A fantastic book that seeks to achieve an important mission. Educating our children on the benefits of eating well, both for their health and the sustainability of the planet. Well done Hazel!"

Dr. Rupy Aujla, The Doctor's Kitchen.

Published by Grans Guides

www.gransguides.co.uk
Instagram: grans_guides

ISBN 978-1-7398557-0-3

Illustration by Emily Cox
Design by Pearl Sun

GRAN'S GUIDE TO
GOOD GUTS

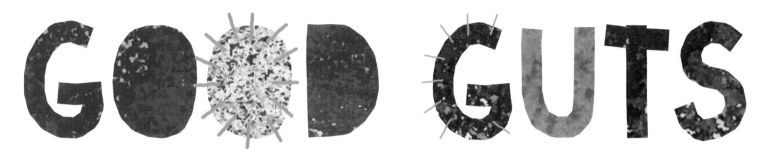

My Friend Mikey

Written by
Hazel Gaydon

Illustrated by
Emily Cox

GRAN'S GUIDE TO GOOD GUTS

My Friend Mikey

INTRODUCTION

For those who will use this book to help the children they care about

One thing we would all want for our children is that they stay healthy in order to live their best life. Science has shown, through multiple studies, the vital importance of guarding our gut health. The microbiome is probably the most important part of us for which we must take care. Its role is extraordinary in influencing most chronic illnesses of the western world, many of which are at epidemic levels now.

If we do not wake up to this, we could contribute inadvertently to our children's future struggles in mental and physical health. The younger they learn and understand the principles for themselves, the better choices they can make. As Frederick Douglass, the social reformer, is quoted as saying: 'It is easier to build strong children than to repair broken men.'

I write this book for all parents, teachers, health professionals and other carers who share my hopes. It is best for children to read it in the company of an adult so that discussion may follow. It would be ideal for a home or classroom project, dovetailing with other material in a health module. There are worksheets at the back if you would like to create further ways to make the most out of the story.

We live in a wonderful world designed for our well-being and pleasure; we inhabit wonderful bodies designed to work well if we treat them right. I hope you will be inspired to celebrate both our world and our health as you use this book with the children you know.

As I complete the book, the world has come through several lockdowns caused by a virus pandemic. As we adjust to living with the imminence of viral infections, what better time to ensure that our children do not become the vulnerable adults with 'underlying health conditions' who succumb most easily. Let them be the resilient ones because they chose the best diet and lifestyle in their early years.

Introduce them to Mikey in this book and he will help to lead the way!

Hazel Gaydon
East Sussex
2023

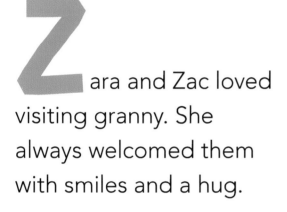

Zara and Zac loved visiting granny. She always welcomed them with smiles and a hug.

Each time she was prepared and had planned lots of activities. The children knew she was sometimes in pain but she was cheerful and never complained.

Most of all she was lots of fun, they nicknamed her **FG: Fun Gran!** Especially when she took part in the circuit training she set up for their exercise sessions.

FG would FLY
on her swing.

FG would BOUNCE
on her mini
trampoline.

FG would SWIVEL with her hula hoop.

FG would SHIVER and SHAKE on her wobble machine. The children loved this best as it made all their muscles tremble as they stood on the shaking surface.

Watching her bounce and wobble and swing, it is no wonder that Zac asked 'FG, why don't you need a rest?'

'No way Zac, I'm only in my seventies!' and they all laughed. 'I do sit down once you've gone home though'.

'Let me tell you why I'm keeping fit' said Gran.

'Last time I was in hospital, I made a big decision. I want to learn everything I can to keep strong and stay active as I get older. So, I did loads of homework - a bit like you do when you have a project at school. Then I talked to my doctor; I have learnt lots of really interesting things. Best of all, I have found a new friend.'

'Do we know your new friend?' Zara asked.

'Now this will surprise you' said Gran. 'He's not just my friend, he is your friend too. Actually he is everyone's friend, he knows us inside out and his name is **Mikey**.'

'Whoa, I don't get this Gran.' Zac was puzzled.

'How can that be true?'

Meet Mikey

'Scientists have found that we have a whole system of living things inside us. They are in every part of us but mostly in our gut' said Gran patting her tummy. We never see them, but they are there from the moment we are born.

Mikey is the name I have given that system.

The proper name for this is **Microbiome**, but Mikey seems more friendly'.

'So what is he doing inside us?' Zara didn't much like the sound of it.

Gran explained: 'It's like this. Our own bodies are made of millions of things we call 'cells'. There are lots of different types, each doing a different job. They all make our bodies work.

Mikey has trillions of cells, even more than we do. His cells have names like bacteria and fungi and viruses. We call them **micro-organisms**. Because they are so tiny we would never know they are there. They do an incredible job, they turn our food into all the things our bodies need to keep us well.

'Are you keeping up with me so far?' Gran laughed.

blood cells

skin cells

stem cells

bone cells

'Come on, I've got some pictures to show you' Gran took them to sit at the table.

'Oh isn't **Mikey** sweet Gran, are they his micro-organisms inside?' Zara was learning fast.

'Listen, this is the brilliant thing about **Mikey**. If his micro-organisms are well and happy, he can organise things inside us to keep us feeling great. **He is like our own private doctor inside!** If not we can feel unwell or out of sorts. Thankfully, we can help **Mikey** do his job'.

The children wanted to know how that works.

'It works when we are careful about the choices we make. Do you know what keeps us healthy and strong?'.

'Mum says it's fresh air and exercise' Zara smiled.

'That's true, but nothing is more important than what we eat or drink. **Mikey** loves good food, but some foods make him struggle; then he can't help us.'

Gran showed them a picture of **Mikey** eating.

NATURAL FOODS

give him
power
and
energy.

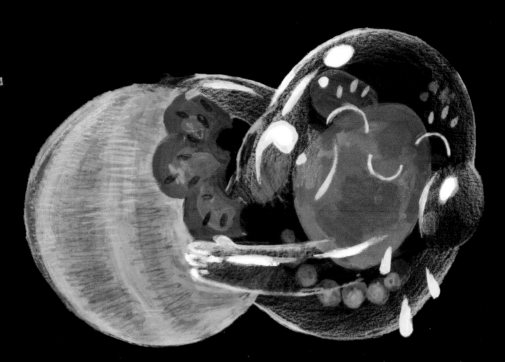

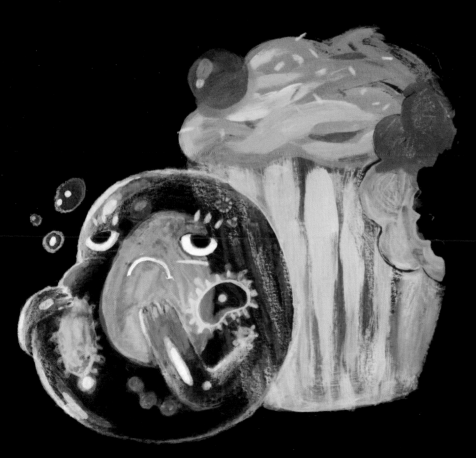

PROCESSED FOODS

make him
weak.

'He has some favourites which I try to eat a lot' said Gran. '**Fibre** is top of his list'.

'That doesn't sound very nice' Zac wished it was time for a snack.

'Let's have some tasty fibre right now' said Gran, and she gave them each an **apple** to enjoy.

Our bodies need **nutrients** from things called **proteins, fats** and **carbohydrates, vitamins** and **minerals;** these all come in the plants and grains we eat. **Nature provides them!** Fibre is in all foods that grow; it makes sure the food we eat goes smoothly on its journey through us.

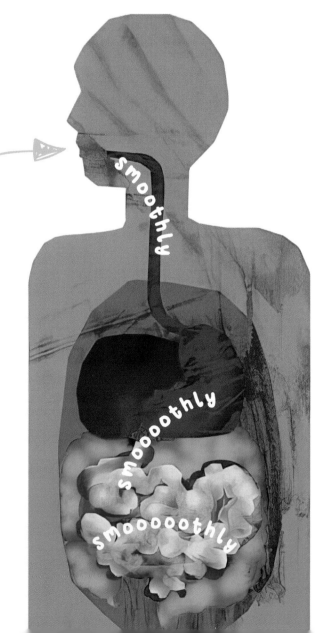

That journey is called our digestive system. It starts when we chew our food and takes it to our tummies and **Mikey's** system is waiting to turn the food into what we need.

Let's look at some of **Mikey's** best foods.

'Mikey loves colourful vegetables. He thinks they are out of this world!'

Which ones do you like to eat?

Onion

Ginger

Leeks

Red cabbage

Beetroot

Carrots

Garlic

Tomatoes

Sweet potatoes

Peppers

'My best ones are **beetroots** and **carrots**', Zara said.

Zac said, '*I tried pickled red cabbage at Christmas and it was really crunchy; but my choice would be* **sweetcorn** *and* **broccoli**'.

Gran said, '*I know you both love to eat fruit. That will make* Mikey *very happy. You could tick off all the fruit you have enjoyed.*'

'*Gran, does that mean we only can eat vegetables and fruit?*' the children wanted to know.

'Oh, no dears, there are so many tasty choices to enjoy. Other foods Mikey loves include **beans** and **grains** and **nuts** and **seeds** and **herbs** and **spices**. Have a look at my herb and spice drawer'.

Zara wanted to play with all the little jars and packets.

'We can do that another day,' promised Gran. 'But for now just smell these fresh herbs on my window sill'.

So, now you know a lot about what Mikey needs to keep him happy.

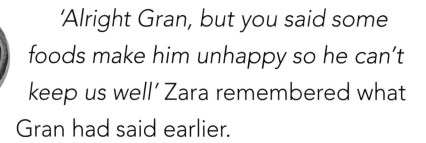

'Alright Gran, but you said some foods make him unhappy so he can't keep us well' Zara remembered what Gran had said earlier.

Gran took a deep breath. 'This bit may be hard to hear but it is really, really important. It's the S word, can you guess what that might be? It is SUGAR'.

'Not the type in fruit because that is natural, I'm talking about PROCESSED SUGAR; the type that is added to factory food and sweet treats. This gives Mikey a hard time.'

'Oh yes, is that what your poster means on the wall?'

'Well spotted Zara, I have it there to remind me about Mikey and my plan to stay well. You see, factory foods usually contain things called 'ADDITIVES' and they upset Mikey too.'

If it came from a plant, eat it.

If it was made in a plant, don't eat it.

'Too many sugary foods and additives will make the bad micro-organisms have a fight with the good ones. Did you know that was going on inside you?'

17

'I've got an idea you two, on another visit we can play food detectives. We will go to a supermarket and spot the foods Mikey loves and hates. We can easily tell when we read the labels; I can explain more about that when we are there. Then we will buy things we can enjoy as well as Mikey.'

'Can we have clipboards and pencils?' Zara wanted to be a proper detective.

Gran decided they had learnt enough for one day, it was time to make lunch. The children loved helping her to cook. It seemed strange to use vegetables and fruit to make cakes, but Gran was sure they'd like the **beetroot** and **apple brownies** with **avocado icing**. Their fingers turned red when they grated the beetroot.

Then they mixed up all the ingredients for **Brilliant Bean Burgers**. Gran used **frozen vegetables** for these.

'They are just as good for you,' she told them. Once they had cooked them they all picked **lettuce** and **tomatoes** from the garden to make a salad. There were **orange** and **banana** slices to finish the meal.

'Gran there is something I don't understand,' Zara was feeling a little bit annoyed.

'You said that we have to stay well and strong; but **I am** *well and* **I am** *strong and* **I'm the fastest runner in my class***'.

'I know Zara, you were brilliant at sports day. I was cheering.' Gran smiled as she remembered it.

'At the moment you are young and strong and your body is working well for you, but if you keep making **Mikey** fight the battles inside, one day he won't be able to win.'

'Later in your life you might start to see some signs; you might feel **TIRED**, or put on **WEIGHT** or get in **BAD MOODS** or **NOT BE ABLE TO THINK CLEARLY**.'

'It might show up as **PAIN** or you might feel **ANXIOUS**; some people get **ITCHY SKIN**. So much about when you are older depends on how **Mikey** can protect you now.'

'I'm older now and even so, I'm trying to do what I can, so I swim and I do the activities we share when you come to visit. **Most of all I'm very careful about what I eat**.'

'So do we have to carry on helping **Mikey** until we are your age?' Zac was concerned.

'Zac, you and Zara will benefit if you do, we all have to be careful as long as we live. If **Mikey** is strong, we can enjoy life so much more.'

After their yummy lunch the children packed the rest of the brownies to take home.

'Mum will love these,' they both agreed.

'Yes, but will Mikey love what we have eaten today?' Zara was still trying work it out.

'The food you helped to make today will have made Mikey fitter than ever,' Gran was sure about that.

'So everyone is **happy**,' Zara called out as she ran to have a last turn on the swing.

'Don't forget we're doing food detectives next time Gran.' Zac heard mum's car. 'Can we tell mum about Mikey?'

'Tell everyone you can, let's try to help lots of people to **stay well and enjoy life**'.

Gran waved until they were out of sight. She had a few more minutes on the wobble machine before she settled down for the evening.

'It is such good **fun** being a Gran', she smiled to herself.

APPENDIX

WORKSHEETS

These are intended for:

- **Teachers** who may choose to make this book the basis for a classroom project

- **Parents** or grandparents who may base some family activities around this book.

- **Doctors** or health coaches who may find the material helpful for community groups or education sessions

- **Children** who have become interested in the information and would enjoy testing themselves.

These worksheets can be copied for use in home or school projects, but make sure they are used as an add-on to this book in order for them to make sense and underline the teaching points.

ROVING REPORTER

A reporter goes to meet people to get information. Today, you are the reporter. You are going to find two grown-up people you know. It could be a grandparent, or a family friend or someone who helps at school. Your parent or teacher can help you choose the people.

Explain that you are writing a report on staying healthy. Take this book with you to show them why you are interested. Ask them if they would be willing to answer a few questions and write down their answers.

Use the information you have gathered, to write a report about each person you asked. Finish your report with a suggestion for each of them about how they can help Mikey for themselves.

1. Do you think you are in good health for your age?

2. Do you take any tablets for a medical condition?

3. Did you know about 'My Friend Mikey' before seeing this book?

4. Are you able to do any exercise? What exercise do you enjoy?

5. Do you eat lots of fruit and vegetables? What are your favourites?

6. Do you have lots of friends and family?

7. What advice would you give me about staying healthy?

GRAN'S GUIDE BY HAZEL GAYDON

QUESTIONS AND ANSWERS

See if you can match the right answer to each question.

Draw a line to link them.

What are probiotics?

Why does Mikey live inside us?

What goes wrong if we eat too much sugar?

Can you ever eat foods that are made in a factory?

Why should we eat green vegetables every day?

Mikey controls the balance of bacteria in our gut to keep us well

They are friendly bacteria for our gut

The bad bugs start winning and Mikey gets weak

They give Mikey his favourite nutrients to keep him strong

If you check labels to find harmful chemicals or pesticides

GRAN'S GUIDE BY HAZEL GAYDON

MAKE A MEAL FOR MIKEY

Choose from all the foods that Mikey loves and create a delicious meal to make him strong.

Draw the foods you choose on each section.

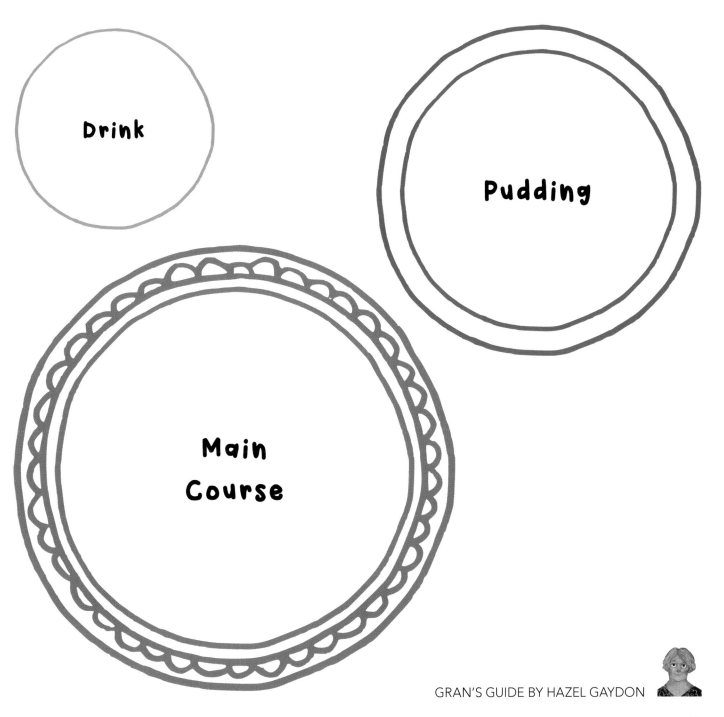

Drink

Pudding

Main Course

FOODS THAT MAKE YOU STRONG

Can you find foods that make Mikey strong?
Colour them in to make them stand out.

FOOD DETECTIVES

On a visit to the shops, take time to look at the labels on foods. Some foods have been altered (processed) to change the colour or flavour or to keep them on sale longer. These 'additives' are not all bad, but you shouldn't eat a lot of them.

Some should be avoided completely including:

1. **Sodium nitrites**
2. **Sulphites**
3. **Trans fats**
4. **Monosodium glutamate**
5. **Artificial food colours or flavours**
6. **High fructose corn syrup**
7. **Sodium benzoate**
8. **Canola oil**

Also, avoid any foods with ingredients your Mum can't pronounce! They may have hidden chemicals that can be harmful.

The amount of sugar is also a key thing to check.

Source: The Association of UK Dieticians

GRAN'S GUIDE BY HAZEL GAYDON

HEALTHY SWAPS

Try some of these to see how fast you can help Mikey.

White potatoes → change for sweet potatoes

White rice  → change for cauliflower rice

Fruit juice → change to eating a piece of fruit

Fizzy drinks  → change to sparkling water with some real fruit juice

White bread → change to wholegrain bread or corn cakes

Breakfast cereal → change to oatmeal, smoothies, yogurt with berries

Bought treats → change to home-made treats with healthier ingredients

Always going out in the car 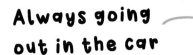 → change to walking when you can

Watching TV → change to outdoor activities to get some fresh air

Make life fun and stay healthy at the same time!

Sweet potato created by Icons Producer, rice by Amina Manukyan, fruit by Eucalyp, soda by Orin zuu, bread by P Thanga Vignesh, cereal by Claire Skelly, cupcake by Econceptive, car by Lars Meiertoberens and swing by Danishicon from the Noun Project

 GRAN'S GUIDE BY HAZEL GAYDON

THE MAGIC OF MOVING

Choose your favourite exercises and try to do 30 minutes every day.

- Walking
- Running
- Hopping
- Workout programmes.

- Trampolining
- Skipping
- Stretching

Save our world

Care for the planet as well as your health. Use water wisely. Read labels to avoid chemicals. Reduce plastics when possible.

FG's FRUITY GREEN FIX

This is what Gran drinks to energise her:

- 1 apple
- Handful of spinach
- Handful of Kale
- 5 pineapple chunks
- 2 inches of cucumber
- 1 stalk of celery
- Half a peeled lemon
- Half an avocado
- 1 carrot
- 1 cup of berries

Chop everything. Blend with a large cup of coconut water for 40 seconds. Enjoy!

This book is dedicated to my grandchildren:

Zac, Liza

Molly, Reuben, Stanley,

Martha, Elsie, (Florence – always loved, never forgotten), Zebedee,

Phoenix and Lotus

Acknowledgements

Working with Emily, a budding new illustrator and creative designer Pearl Sun has been fun; Maddy Glenn of SWS-publishing has been invaluable as my editor as has Carl Thompson on formatting; so my warm thanks to each of them. Thanks also to my focus groups, my grandchildren and my husband for their helpful comments, the final form of the story owes a lot to you all.

My passion for this subject was fired by several forward-thinking doctors who inspired me to study the whole area of helping oneself to better health. Dr.Rangan Chatterjee, Dr.Rupy Aujla and Sir Muir Gray, were all kind enough to be interviewed by me on my radio programme for Age UK on 'Staying Well as you get Older'. Virginia Harper whom I met in USA, saw the potential of the book in her work with digestive illnesses and was enthusiastic for me to produce it. Dr. Michael Greger encouraged me to 'Get that book published!' and I am indebted to him for Nutrition Facts, the site I refer to frequently and which keeps me up to date. I have one of the finest GPs in Sussex who understands my antipathy to 'a pill for every ill' and has always offered the best support – thanks Adrian! My thanks to many in the functional medicine world for making vital information on the latest science accessible to everyone, thus helping to change the face of healthcare delivery as well as to bring hope for all to thrive, whatever our age or stage.

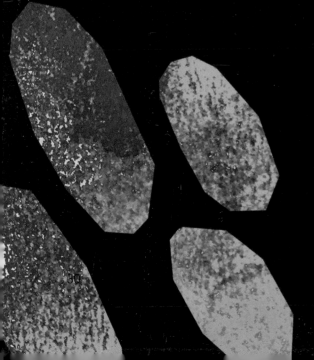
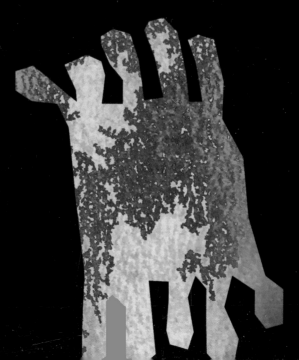
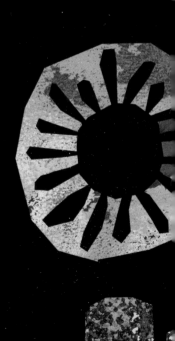